5.75

Fall by Fury

FALL
BY
FURY
& OTHER MAKINGS

EARLE BIRNEY

McCLELLAND AND STEWART

The Canadian Publishers
McClelland and Stewart Limited
25 Hollinger Road, Toronto   M4B 3G2

Other Books in Print
available from McClelland and Stewart Limited

Collected Poems, 2 volumes
The Damnation of Vancouver
Down the Long Table
Ghost in the Wheels, Selected Poems
Turvey

The Cow Jumped Over the Moon,
available from the author

CANADIAN CATALOGUING IN PUBLICATION DATA

Birney, Earle, 1904-
  Fall by fury

Poems.

ISBN 0-7710-1430-9 pa.

I. Title.

PS8503.I7F35   C811'.5'4   C78-001305-0
PR9199.3.B58F35

Printed and Bound in Canada

This book is for Wai-lan

"Though we cannot make our sun
Stand still, yet we will make him run"

Contents

1
SKIN DIVERS

fall by Fury

Now was the season
summer so high and still
the birds in the circling woods
held all the tale

Past deserted nests I rose
through a world of web
severing   dropping the black treebones
for the consummation of winter fire
O through the brace and embrace
of a hundred living arms I swung
gathering delight in my own ease
muscle and breath at a play of skill

I was climbing the tall beech
to prune dead limbs
that overhung the summer home
before some gale might hurl
a snag into glass

Each grasp tugged at the old zest
for a climb: the rock-fort a year back
in Sri Lanka   and before   in my sixties
up the yellow spines of the Olgas. . .
at fifty-eight in cloud on the ribs
of Huayna Picchu. . .at thirty
inching down chalk on Lulworth cliffs
. . .twenty-one and over the icy necks
of the Garibaldis. . .and before that
the mountains of youth. . .Temple. . .Edith
all the climbings made in joy of the sport
and never with hurt

as now to the topmost vault
of the beechtree's leaves I rose
to the flooding memories of childhood
perched in my first treehouse
safe in its green womb

Where brittle branches had threatened
a tunnel of light shone up to me now
as I sat in the secrets of leaf
and smiled on the innocent roof
that hid my love preparing our meal

Shining ahead was the fortnight
given us here alone by our friends
to swim with the small fish in the pond
read and doze in the sun
hide in salal to watch the fox by their den
or to work with hands on wood
and heart on words
rhythms already shaping themselves
in the piney air this first of the mornings

So I threw the last snag down
and the locked saw after
turning and shifting my grips
to descend to Wai-lan
when something   my Hubris
some Fury of insect wing and sting
drove its whining hate at my eye
One hand unloosed convulsive to shield
and I slipped
forever from treetops

Caught in a yielding chair of air
I grasped and grasped at a speeding reel
of branches half-seized and wrenched away
by the mastering will of the earth
The next bough surely —
                              my hard mother
crushed me limp in her stone embrace
stretched me still with the other limbs
laid my cloven hip and thigh
with those I had cleft

And that was a world and two summers ago
yet still in the night I reach
for holds eluding my clutch
till the moment comes when the Furies
relent   I catch and cling
swoop   alight on a friendly ground
and run again on two good feet
over the grass of dream

Toronto, 1977

anthropologists from the Black Hole

Glint of motion
on the coloured tablecloth —
something black and so small
i can just make out it's
an ant   no   a team of *hormigas*
the first I've seen in my Mexican house
They're lugging a bread crumb
bigger than they are
headfirst down the tableleg's precipice

Such speed such invisible strength!
Imagine descending in minutes
a thousand vertical metres
without ropes or a piton
and packing a barrel of flour
Already the pair has reached the great tile plain
and pausing only to shift holds
it's across and challenging
the blank wall of my basement kitchen

With an effort I turn from watching
and make my morning trip to the post office

Returning I see now there are hundreds
of these infinitesimal beings
rippling out and back in utter silence
across the remotest wastes of the house
I brew coffee and bring my cup to the table
It rattles   I feel huge and clumsy
But I know their silence is false
The air twangs with secrets
beyond the kiloherz range of my ears
My home is replaced by their newfound continent
where I'm not even noticed
unless as a drifting of cloud
passing harmless   so far

I get up and search their wall
Yes   they are all wriggling out from a single hole
high in the plasterface
and glistening down a narrowing crack
that ends at the overhang of the baseboard
Here they clamber down to the perilous flatlands

The boldest radiate off then
zigzag explorers unravelling all my deserts
but most are heaving up the table spire
to whatever trove lurks on my *mesa*
And all this time they are bumping
dodging passing overpassing
and exchanging cryptic head-taps
with the returning vanguard
laden now but retracing with equal fidelity
the same impossible route
from my cotton savannahs down to the plain
and up to their dark cave in my wall

What are they dragging back   these mortals
to their own world
on the other side of my moon?

The telephone calls me away
and I tramp out for my Spanish lesson
But the ants are into my head now
and soon I am back   armed with a pocket lens
and determined to walk in the Lilliput
they conduct still in my kitchen

Nothing at first surprises
Some labour in pairs with a grain
of polished rice
or a crystal of sugar
And here on the floor a threesome
is pushing and pulling an oatmeal flake
striped like a Masai warrior's shield

But they do not live by bread alone
One bears proudly
a fleck of straw from a broom
another a snippet of thread
and the wall-crack is flecked
with bits of paper moving upwards

What of these others who range the farthest
over the barren tiles and the cliffs of madera?
Why do they push blindly
past delectable tidbits
in a tremor of search and rejection
stopping each other to quiver
antennae signals and tappings   and smells
of who-knows-what and scurrying
back to their alpine catacomb
with all six hands quite empty?

I must leave them again
to water my plants in the patio
and fetch the noon paper.
Quickly I slip back
to peer once more like a god on their busyness
— but they are gone
every last glint of them
vanished forever
down their mysterious galleries

I feel immensely let down
and walk about in my vast moon crater
an abandoned Cyclops   restless
wanting to follow

Worse than abandoned — I was never discovered
For surely the first time they came
rivering out through their tunnel
and pouring down the long limestone canyon
they were looking for somebody else

I think of the Olduvai Gorge
which channelled itself unheeded
while ten thousand generations of Africans
hurried above the sunken cliffs
to pursue the antelope over the grasslands
and alert for slavers and slaves
Two centuries then of Karamoja Bells
and Teddy Roosevelts and Hemingways
followed them over the blue horizons
to shoot the biggest possible creatures —
that later proved only half the size
of the super-rhinoceros   the archetypal bull
or the dinotherian jumbo
lurking a few metres under their boots

Even Professor Kattwinkel   lepidopterist
clambering up from the gorge's mouth
discovered the giant bones
only by slipping and falling back on them
while reaching to net an unusual butterfly

It took twenty more years and a Leakey
to spot the sharpened stones and the brainpans
of the genus that did them all in
along with itself perhaps   and us eventually
(the hunters hunted
the lost and the found and the finders together)

I peer up the tiny cave in the wall of my kitchen
Somewhere on its mirror side this moment
those ants have their own family of Leakeys
their anthropologists
tireless in directing the sorting labelling dating
delicate brushing and reconstructing
of their grand primeval ancestors

What crafty and strange progenitors
to have wrought such polished monoliths of rice!
How subtle and strange their great-ants
to have hidden their formic treasures
in cryptic codex and stela
among dazzling fields of inedible string
on the levelled top of a wooden pyramid
towering from deserts of baked clay

I wander my empty kitchen
bothered now by my own nonsense
Why does the fantasy grow too painful?
Granted that all their insect energy
devotion and daring were squandered
collecting mementos of me
whom they cannot conceive —
then they are happy as beings can be
for they store wisdom never to be discredited
(and some of it succulent)

It's more than the ants that bemuse me
whose flickering expeditions
could end with the spray can
the anxious housemaid has put in my hand
Perhaps it's the rough globe I ride on
the pellet that's rolled by that starry procession
of ceaseless finders and keepers
who bear all artifacts back at last
to the black irreversible holes in space

On my lunar floor some shadow grows
of a Cloud
weaponed and watching

San Miguel Allende, April 1975

birthday

Some nine hundred fifty circlings of my moon
i doubt i'll see a thousand
my face lunar now too
strings of my limbs unravelled
trunk weak at the core   like an elm's

worse   the brain's chemistry out of kilter
memory a frayed net
speech a slowing disc the needle jumps

& yet i limp about   insist in fact
on thanking the sky's pale dolphin
for flushing & plumping herself once more
into a pumpkin —
that storybook Moon still in my child mind
too deep for any astronaut to dig out

& stubbornly i praise the Enormous Twist
that set my sun to spinning me
these 26,663 times on the only known planet
that could sprout me

i praise too the great god Luck
that grew me into health
(out of mumps, chicken pox, measles, pneumonia, scarlet
fever, enteritis & a dozen broken bones)
Luck that freed me to roam & write
that gave me a lifetime of friends

some dawns it's true came up with betrayal
failure   rejection   bombs dropping
they taught me only happiness had been
& could be again

Sophocles said it's better not to be born
but he waited till 90 to tell us
at 74 i'm too young to know

so i bless whatever stars
gave me a cheerful father
with a bold heart & a dancing body
who passed me his quick eye & ear
& his faithful love-affair with words

& how can i not be grateful
to a Universe that made
my most enduring mother?
she too valued Luck   but she bet on Pluck
If ever deed of mine achieved
a glint of the unselfish
it was a fallen spark
from her lifetime's fire

when i give my dust to the wind
it will be with thanks
for those fellow earthlings
who forgave or forgot
my onetime wife   our son   our grandsons
& those comrades who held me
steady on cliffs

above all
my gratitude to whatever Is above all
to the young who light my evening sky
& to her   my happiest Happenstance —
if she remember me with love
when she is old
it will be immortality enough

2
THE PERFECT CANADIANS

MAD/MOD/ODD/AD/MAN

a day with the toronto day-lies
(a daycollage of the real news back in our centennial year)

Two psychiatrists have cured 16 women of frigidity.
Call these beasts off! I'll do anything you say!
      In silence she suffered,
      In patience she bore
"A Sane View on Sex" at both services
Deserted husbands & wives! Let's get together!
What's Better Than One Shield?
Tooniks by Inook Co. Ltd. at Frobisher Bay.
U.S. DELEGATES WALK OUT ON CUBANS AT U.N.
watch the sparrow-sized pipits bobbing as they walk.
The Intelligent Person's guide to Mate Hunting.
Two! And Only Kotex Napkins Have Two!
      In the midst of our sorrow
      Bladder Irritation May Disturb Sleep
SELL OUR WATER & GET NEW INDUSTRIES
Over-tipping gets you nowhere.
      A dear husband, dad and grandpa
Most Frobisher Eskimos live on relief.
Tooniks Replace Ookpiks for Expo 67.
It's a company not a co-op.
Color makes all the commercials magical,
I adore them all, black, yellow, white, French,
so long as they are blondes, the singer said.
Estee Lauder's Lip Gloss Comes in Frosted Peach.
Christians come but once a year.
No Eskimo living has ever seen a Toonik
but it's a good year for movie nuns;
Virgo! You can break new emotional ground today!
LOVE SAYS "NOW" — See the rings at Morse tomorrow!
Of course "The Singing Nun" can bring uplift too
& Free Space-Shield Eye-Protectors.
ANOTHER ARCTIC DOLL FOR MARKET.
Baby face you punch me. Write me quick.
So what if it's only a highschool hootenanny
      Loving thoughts shall ever wander
      To the spot where she was laid.

Will anyone knowing her whereabouts
meet Sedlock the only Kabloona making Tooniks for Inook.
Lake Titicaca's Moonlight Cruise Attracts Canadians
TAURUS: it might be best to stay close to home —
but your all-inclusive budget holiday includes
one cocktail, dinner, floorshow at the Ritz, and
the area's top quarterbacks, who are meeting
at the City Hall in a United Appeal
passing contest CATS CHOICE TO TAME LIONS
Hear Pastor Vaters: Let's Use Force. The Christian Hour.
"Christ was insane", he told his Sunday School
"No one has ever photographed a woman's body
with more devotion", "I expect everyone
to be busy enjoying it", said Brenda Gilk.
"Sorry I had to hit you with my shoe, Mr. Brannan."
DIEF CLOBBERS THE PEACE HECKLERS
             But many a silent tear is shed
             When others are asleep
Mr. Bribery didn't you hear me?
An abominable snowpik   throws a football fartest.
There's more to Hawaii than girls —
CREE CHIEF PREDICTS INDIAN RACE RIOTS TOO

It's all an audacious venture in controlled commotion
& total theatre

U. of Toronto, 1967

gourmet

A circus lion   restless for his turn
slipped from his cage into the biggest tent
A woman screamed   the lion sniffed
eight thousand humans rioted   and went
Two died and seventy-three were hospitalized
The great cat watched   holding his tail
politely still   then romped back to his cage
The meat smelled better in his jail

Old Brompton Road, July 1977

Fifty years of love goddesses

eautifully diffe
est shipment
ay at Toronto's
liers from Europe
Lighting Centre.

ctor MacDea
win by a Star report-
ulted: "My God, that's
good news!"

There's more to Hawa
than girls and Waikik

North Beach (sometime
called "Little Italy")
where the nightlife is—wit

ey have cured 1 ot irigiaity by th
use of LSD in combination with

safest, most comfortable napki

SKIN H
arrow e t
bs as it wal

me. Fo at counts is
women, de n'im-
porte q e; je ne suis
pas rad adore them
all whe are Ameri-
can Eng nch, white,
black or
"Yes, as
they're

Into the sheik's te
comes Valentino, the she
himself, bearing
Agnes A

brought
here?
And he replies,
browed: "Are you n
an enough to know?

nother Arctic d for market

7:

What's better tha e d?

SPECIAL HONEYMOON
SEE AND DO — ALL

OT HINGS TO
ALKING DISTANCE

Potato fu
climb in N.Y.
amid frenzy

Love Says,
"Now

BE SURE TO ATTEND HEDRAL
AMPLE PARKING — N PROVIDED
High-toned sc

e rings at Morse. Our go ave a
of making diamond rings ual as
ve is … Like this wrap l pair

But they usually ck to Kotex.

Eski o hope. Toonik

Cats choice
o tame Lion

CALL THESE BEASTS
OFF! I'LL DO
ANYTHING YOU
SAY!

(only Kotex napkins hav o!)

here is brightness, and rhythm, yet the
till comes through. If you like choruses wit
clusive safeguard shield to provide even abso

Free List Suspended

But the Eskimos
Island are betting
own local creation t
the exotic doll field.

shotgun marriage without shotguns: the rugging & the moving times. by John Todd[1]

(recalling the joint banquet at York Factory trading post, held in 1821 by the furhunters of the Hudson's Bay and Northwest Companies to solemnize the news of the amalgamation already effected in England)

That formidable band of breached Highlanders,
defeated heroes of the opposition,
the Nor-West partners, by no means humbled,
stalked about the old dilapidated fort
on the bleak banks of York Factory
with haughty air and independent step.
When the bell summoned us to dinner
in walked the heterogeneous mass
in perfect silence
& with the utmost gravity.
Like that incongruous animal
seen by the King of Babylon,
one part iron, another of clay,
though joined together
they would not amalgamate.

That crafty fox, George Simpson,[2]
with his usual dexterity in bows & smiles
got them slowly mingling
& to their appointed places.
Some, however, found themselves misplaced.

Directly in front of McIntosh,
he of the shifting black eyes,
sat his enemy, the pompous John Clark.
At the end of a long day's march on snowshoes
the previous winter, they had ended an argument
by a round of pistol shots
deliberately discharged at each other
over the bright blaze of their camp fire,
separated merely by the burning element. . . .

Ah, those were the rugging and the moving times!
The more flexible McIntosh was now persuaded
into a distant seat
But he whom they called Blind McDonnel
found himself directly in front
of his mortal foe of Swan River,
Chief Factor Kennedy.
They had hacked & slashed at each other
with naked swords, & one of them
still bore the marks on his face, — the other,
it was said, — on some less conspicuous part. . . .

I shall never forget the look of scorn
& utter defiance with which their eyes met.
The Highlander snorted, squirted,
& spat between his legs
as restless on his chair
as on a hillock of ants. . . .

I thought it fortunate
they were all without arms.

---

[1] Slightly rearranged and shortened. John Todd was a member of the Committee of Management of the British section of the Hudson's Bay Company west of the Rockies and, after 1851, a member with James Douglas, of the governing Council of Vancouver's Island. See A. S. Morton, *A History of the Canadian West*, London, 1939.
[2] Head of the HBC in Canada; Governor of Rupert's Land.

TRAWNA TUH BELVUL BY KNAYJIN PSIFIK
(for Ron & Lorna Everson)

Tickets!   Wear yuh goan?   Tickets!   Oshwa?   Upta en
upta *en*   *fa*ren.   Tickets tickets!
Wear you goan Oshwa?   Oh *Ot*wa right dare firs coach
Wear yuh goan?   Trennon?   Upta en
Belleville?   Upta en en en yeah Hurry tup. . . .
Awwwwww *bord*! . . . Aw bord. . . . Bore. . . . *Bord*!

Uhmn hunhun Uhmn Ay du dun   *Day* duh dun
day duh duh *day* duh duh
WACKITY duh duh WACKITY CLAG CLANG duh duh
WANGDITTY KLONG
duh DUB de dub deDUB de dub de DRUB de DRUB
de WANGITY WACKLEDEE GELACK GELACK
DUB de dub de DUB de dub de didee
Dub de Didee   Dub de Didee de didee de dee
past the Guild and blast the mills
and whatta lotta whatta lotta lotta autos lotta autos
o good grayshun land of goshen autos waitin
autos banded by the station for the Go train
on we rush   skirting the bluffs   swirling the roughs
starling the puffs   the smelling the luffs
the luff the lufflee flowers the weeds the flowers
the weeds in the ditch   always a ditch
tall with weeds and full of shitch
that fits a ditch but not the flowers
bowers in the whitch?   towers of kitsch   flowers for rich
KLANITY BANG CANG   Can cans in the ditch
no plans for the ditch
log in the ditch   dog by the ditch
dog after bitch   rogue after tits   poles with the ditch
always the poles poles and poles and slow int-oo Whit-
WAKKITY KLANG into what? into Whit into WHIT BEEEEE
Witby!   Ay duh dah duh   fhnn nmmm
Anyone fer Whitby?   Out *this* door
CLANGITY WHAM BonK   clumpity bong. . . .
Awwww BORD. . . .*Bord*!

Uhmn Uhmn Ay dahdun   DAY duh dun day   DAY duh
de died de dee beside the sea beside the LAKE
beside the Lake   beside the see teehee
beside the lakesea   the sealake   and theres a ship
& whats after Whit? apart from a ditch? a scarp on a slake
WALKITY KANG DE DIEDEEAdee   de wen de leevy
O when you leave a   tittle station and
goo cheevin hoo the nation   wen you leaf a leetle patience
and go chuggin thru the marmacans so buggin to
the marmaland go joggin thru the marmalade the BOOOOoo
the bish the bird the bush the bard the bosh
the birch the barm the farm alarm the harm
the barn the barmy farmlands   the squirmy wormlands
where there arent so many farmers   not a farmhand not a —
dots of oil tanks lots of gravel   pots of houses all alike
theres a factory making tractories   baking trucks and
faking cars and tracks and lime and making time
may king sweat shirts may king time and grime and dimes
making making making hay
nnnwrOOOOO. . . .oooooo oo de DEB de didy
DUB de did Dud de OSHee dub de OSHAWA!   Oshwaaa
Ay de fnnm KLANG ITY bumMM   step down . . .
Boy up   Mombaby up

. . . .Awla*bord!*. . . .KLANGITY. . . .Ay de fnnnm de diddle
de drub de drub de WAMGOTY WACKITY
Dob de doe de dub de boe de Boe de BOWMANVILLE
Bowmanville Bowmanville that was Bowmanville
that was Bow-Diddety *dee* ditty *ded* daddy de
KRANG GRANDKIXIG day klasses   baby dozes   boy doesnt
de kassay de hiss-hissy de kaskastle
bluecattle NEW CASTLE newcastle   WAKKITY CLANG

de diddy de diddy de ho de SHUT THAT DOOR de did
SHLANGGG the door the pore and on for more
and more and for pore for port and for whore for Port
PORT HOPE was *Porthope* that wasnt a stop no stop at hope
no hope you dope to port to lope KLAND DE DUPpity
and wheeeee the train goes round the corner
wheee the corner goes round the train
goes BANGLE the trains not round the train has angles
whangles every coach is angled different
angle bangle wrangle seats are jangled sideways dangled
bags jerked bags of the jerks fall in aisles   whumph
HWAAAH   WAWWAWA baby's waking baby's squawking
stuff him a bottle stiff him a battle stop the blattle
blittle   glub glub   blissful   baby blissful
smallboy jealous   ballboy jailsus   mauls his ma
FOOOOO!   food he wants but Maw is nauseous
offspring sprongs and ransacks baskets biscuits
dippity dup the train is dubbiting huppity slowing
dub-a-dee SCREECH   KLANGITY KLANG de KLOE de COE
*Coeburg!. . .*Coeburgawlabord   stepdown   KLANGITY
BOMP   huroo de boy departs and WAW aw waa de bay
de baby de mom dey all stepdown depart de hooo de ray
abord!   Awwww-bord bord

Now we're leaving little Coeburg   feeling hungry
for a Joeburg with a WACKETY BONG an ong an ong
and over the lanes and under the cranes and over
the crows the crows in droves and passing the drains
pass-ing. . .the. . .box. . .cars faster afstrrr   fastrrr
passing th frrrreights and on in the trrrain
passing daisies oxeye daisies foxeyed crazies
on in our train in the rain and the smoke blowing
flowing slowing and into trendy trammelled TRENNON!
Ay de deb—*Trenton nex*   de dub de Trennnnonnn!
KLANGITY   thiswayout   KLONG   BLUmph
   stepdow. . . .*Bord!*

Aw de fnnnhm de diddy de hoede WAKITTY BANG
zipping past th poisonivy   bending out of wendy Trennon
not so trendy not so friendly   Tick-*utts*. . . .Tix please
Wending past the weedy ditches lending eye to randy goat
goat and goatsbeard blueweed white and bindweed blue
once again the curves are angles ANGLE BANGLE
angles trying to be curves   curve to jerk and crurk—
girl is trainsick trainsack shamealack shamble retch
and lake again and gulls and kildeer   crakes and fens
charming stinkweed stinking mayweed purple vetch
mills and poles o see the fleabane mulleins yarrows
sparrows harrows starlings on the poles on the boles

now were sliding into siding sliding   now we're meeting
another train that's passing no it's standing   what!
we're passing   passingpassing who is what is passing
life is passing life is butta   life is buttacuppa
buttacuppas in the ditches cuppa yella butta dream
purple loosestrife yardsan yardsa purpur goosestride
gardensfulls of vetches tufted vetches creamy vetches
mottled vetches wretched thistles bull and thistles sow
thistles nodding thistles scotch   and O Can-a-da
our own our native Thistle   Thistle? WHISTLE!
slowing now past goats in pasture stoats in stoathouse
BELLL! and houses old red brick and climbing ivy
chickens chickening out from us from *our* bellllLL
clothes fly up on cottage closelines   loathlines
boxy flumes with bladder campion   foxy plumes of wild
barley lousewort mousewort dandy lions yellow toadflax
yellow cat's ear streets and elms and BELLLL and
BELLVUL! *Belvulnex*   swayout   De Dub de Dub-bid-dee
whnhmmmm   squee-ik   Bellllllll-KLANGity KLONG
Stepdown. . . .Hi there Ron, hi Lorna

Ontario, July 1977

the perfect canadians

out in every weather
they never complain
taciturn perhaps but honest
& though inclined to live in built-up areas
they love flowers lawns trees
and are friends to the smallest creatures

law-abiding they are never known to rob
fight rape or play pinball
in crowds they form queues
& keep to them
never smoke drink take drugs
will volunteer their names at once
ages war service next of kin
& any opinions they might have
or had
about immortality
now that they are all
in the cemetery

Mt. Pleasant, Toronto, 1977

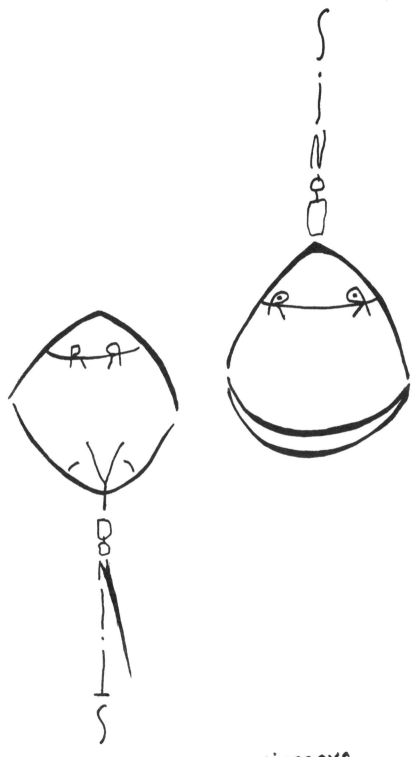

S(T)INBRAYS

plastic plinkles for Gaudy[1] Nite[1½] at HMF[2] College, Yule[3] 1966
(complete with head to foot notes)

Headnotes A

[1]   *Gaudy* OED: a grand feast or entertainment, esp. at an annual college b(r)a(w)ll, fr. L. *gaudium, gaudeo, gaudeass, gaudyhat, gaudeanus, mygog.*

[1½]   *Nite* AS *niht,* as in *nihtgesceort,* nite shirt.

[2]   *HMF:* High Massey-Ferguson College in the University of Toronto.

[3]   *Yule:* AS Geol(a), heathen feast of 12 days at the winter solstice, now known as Kitchmess Holidays. "At Ewle we wanten gambole", *anon* 1589. "Yowle know Ah doan wanna kill no gooks", LBJ, 1966.

Text A: Ancient Roundelay

O teenybop dollies
to hell with tin hollies[1]
& burnable spruces[1] for Ex-miss
Hail acid & crawlies
& sweetgrass[1] & ballies
& rock us away in a kiss-bliss.

Footnotes A

[1]   *Hollies, spruces, grass & kiss-bliss.* The pre-Christian Anglo-Saxons held midwinter rites & lefts to persuade the sun to make his annual swing north again. Available examples of vegetation with green leaves & fruit at midwinter (incl. mistletoe & ivy) decorated the hall as fetishes of fecundity & immortality. The climactic smash was held on Dec. 25 or *Modra Niht* (Mothers' Night)[2], so called because it was the evening during which tribal virgins were at last allowed to get with the fun & fertility. Hence the well-known hymn:

Hark the hairy Angles sung:
Poppa Sun, look how we're hung
With sexy greens & gaudy notions.
So rain down plagues on Danes & Rotions
& grant *us* population explosions

[2]   *Mothers' Night* should not be confused with Mother's Day (Moder Daeg), a later invention of the pagan Oedipals of North America.

Text B: Carol[1]   *God Rust Ye Merry, Gintilemen*

God rust ye merry gintilemen
Let nuthin you dismay
Tamorrah Armabloodygeddon comes
But not on Kitchmess Day
Rev yer moters   salt the snow
Burn the octane high
Smash the bawtles   cut the trees
An let the missuls fly
Like Christ brawt Luv an Peace tadday
Ree-lax man itsa gif
The Bomb aint doo til Bawxn Day —
Is still the Twenny-fit.

Footnote B
Carols. Owing to a series of oversights, Christmas carols were not sung for the first thir-
teen hundred Christmases, which is why we have them sung on radio now as often as
possible.

Text C: Ballad: 8 Nites B4 Xmus

wuz 8 nytes b4 xmus & awl thru the yorkdail shoppn ¢r
evree kreechr wuz byin returnbl gif kooponz
th stawkns wer panteehoz   th chimneez wer gon
& plastik St. Nik wuz lit up on th lon
Th kideez wer nessld with speed by ther telleez
wile vizhns of spaiswar kurdld ther belleez
& mom in hr stretchbelt & mineeskirt ovr
wuz chekn th sittr 2C wuz she sobr
Th moon on th brest uv th nu-falln sno
wuz a hyryzr spotlyt that whisprd HO HO! (Ho Ho ho ho ho)
when what 2 my wondern gaiz shd appeer
but a smal flyn sawsr with inflaytabl deer
& a 3-leggit Pylot who bowd with a leer
"Beri Beri Old Kitch Mess & a Grippy Dew Near!"

Footnote C
St. Nik. St. Niklaas, pronounced *Santa Klaus,* a 3rd C. German Bp. famed for giving
unexpected gifts unobtrusively. Hence it is but a step by way of Teatn Co. & the Trono
Sanna Klaus Prade to the giving of expected gifts obtrusively. In the town of St. Niklaas,
in Belgium, it is the custom of children, on the eve of St. Niklaas day, to fill their clogs
with hay to feed the saint's white horse. In the war winter of 1944, when the author at-
tended this feast in the company of several score Canadian soldiers, there was no hay,
some of the children no longer had clogs, and one little girl no longer had feet, having
skipped onto one of our anti-personnel mines. The gifts were supplied by us: chocolate
bars & vitamin pills from our home parcels, & a ton of coal flogged by our adjutant from
our own Black Market. Since then, of course, we won the war, brought peace on earth,
and all children are warm & well-fed & 2-legged.

Samuel Champlain's first Christmas dinner in Canada included eel stew, baked pigeons, owls, blackbirds, & a deep squirrel pie. But no ale.

Text D: Carol: Bring Us In Good Ale (15C with Canadian accretions)

> Bryng us in no befe, for there is mony bonys
> but bryng us in good ale, for that goth down at onys.
> Bryng us in no dokes flesch, for thei slober in the mer,
> but bryng us squirrels & blackbirds & eels & Carlings
>   ber.
> Bryng us in no bacon, for that is passyng fatte,
> but bryng us in O'Keefe's, & gyf us moch of thatte.
> Bryng us Dow to go well, & bryng us India pale,
> For oure blyssed Lady sak, bryng us in good ale.

Text E: John Audelay's Hymn for Children's Day, c1475
(with one syllable added for updating)

> With al the reverence that we may
> worchip we Childermas Day.
> Christ crid in cradil, "Moder, ba ba!"
> The childer of Asia cridyn "wa, wa!"
> For their mirth it was a-gon
> when Herod fiersly did hem kill,
> sent his knyghtes into the Est
> bearing grene leaves of *na*palm,
> decking mother, burning child,
> till the screaming mouth was filld.

Massey College, Toronto, Dec. 1966

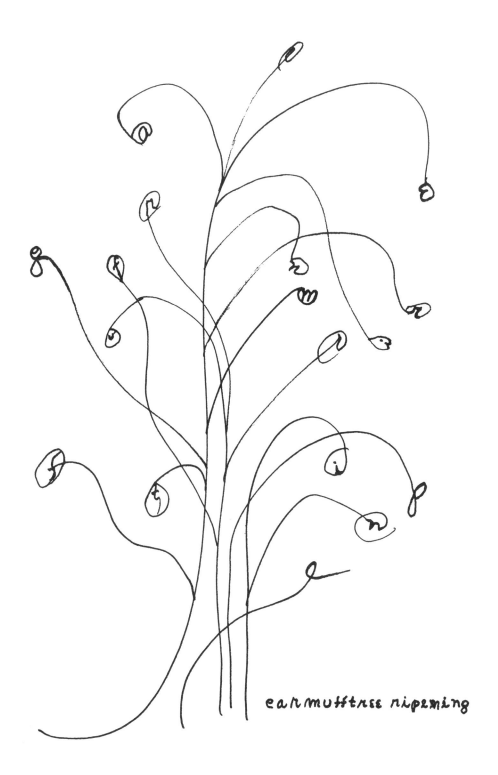

earmufftree ripening

excelsior on the prairies
(for Peter Stevens)

never be lulled
by a prairie's monotony
        February mid-day we walk
        inside an indigestible sandwich
        greywhite sky unbroken above
        anyone's suburb in the middle
        greywhite plain flattened under our feet
        to infinity
wait!   the street gives way to space
        snowcover suddenly drops
        to something bluer
        great pale ice-trapped anaconda
        yes   a river   the great Saskatchewan
        (North or South?   never mind)
look!   down valley live water
        has broken through somehow   steaming
        (it's the waste   says my host
        from that factory across the ravine)
        (but what makes it so hot?   shush!)
        it was -24° C on the radio this morning
        and this town has a boiling canyon and
regard!   at my feet the bare slope has been iced
        (by the kids) they've left cardboard box-tops
        wide enough for even a poet's ass
voila!   the ancient visiting scop
        and the university's resident bard
        aiming above the steam
        are sliding like whirling spiders
        down down to the yet unbroken ice

Saskatoon, 1972

family picnic in Gran Canaria

No rain for seven years
There'll be no rain
on this offshore island of the Sahara
Only dews and sea-mists
bless these horny flowers
where father grips his ancient camera

In the finder is his little daughter
a Spanish curl to the lips
soft as the agave's petals
Cuddled between mama and grandpa
she strains to be still

Under the shining skull
he has bared
the old man is thinking
      this is my granddaughter
      there will be this record
      see already the hips are a woman's

Sidelong the mother watches
a dog curving to the lunch basket
She is told to smile

High and white the sun rides
over the volcano
squeezing their eyes to raisins
Even the child's face wrinkles
in the savage light

The prophetic camera
engraves against the lava slope
the suffering cheeks
the anxious foreheads
Grandfather overexposed
will be death-white
There will be despair in all mouths
hard-ridden by the sun.

Agaete, June 1976

first aid for poets

```
d         .        d
e         .        e
i         .        e
d       t          n
ob      h          es
m        e         o
  e     ibs        t
  s      t e       i
  i                u
  d    fo    mosq
         T   E
         O   B
       arcs  fing
        t ·      · e
        c     ·    r
        h          s
        e          o
        d          f
       tyb      poet
        h           r
        e           y
```

victoria, b.c., 1971

3
FALL IN SPRING

My little chickadee

beginning

the miracle
leaps in the sap unseen
under the scarred elm's bark
to a skyfull of buds

the truth runs
from the old
hands on the keys
to the song in the young throat

the magic flows
in the wind that bends
the waterlily's face
to the lips of the wrinkling lake

uxbridge, 1973

i should have begun with your toes

with maybe just the little one
so clean & succulent
so tiny
it's no toe at all
but a spare nipple   ummmm

now the big one?
big? the nail on it so weeny
& silvery
it's more like a stamp-hinge
to hold down some rarity
a pink imperforate
engraved in *taille douce*

& you've got ten
all in mint condition

& now let's forget
philately
& up the golden stairs!

father grouse

some mornings trying to write
i get like an old ruffed partridge
flopping off & on the nest
scared somebody'll steal
those handsome brown eggs
i've never quite laid yet

flinching from cloud shadows
hearing a fox behind every bush
snakes in the grass
shots on the hill—
limping & trembling around
from what looked like a man
but was only a dumb moose—
till i crumple down beat
with nothing done
& then the phone rings

but listen!
it isnt another mag salesman
or the Poets' League about dues
out of that lovely earpiece
comes a voice spreading sunshine
all through the woods
& i sit back drumming softly
to the loveliest partridge of all
(whose eggs they really are)
& feeling energy-control
right down to my wingtips

after we hang up
quietly i'm warming the eggs again
if i cant lay i can hatch
maybe something of me
will show in the chicks

Alexander St., July 1974

52

coming back from the airport

the flat's not real
a room restored
in a period museum
exact but unconvincing
i do not believe the TV
will turn on

your small slippers
poke from under the chesterfield
something arranged
by a slick director
they do not move
lacking the brown feet
which were human
with minute calluses

i water the chrysanthemum
silent as a photograph
nothing drinks
the armchair
stiff with air

only the bed
grows & is heard
twice as big
petrified with tousling
& yet an imitation too
a stuffed animal
nothing warm under the fur
no
body

Alexander St., Dec. 1973

omnibus

a new city bus she is too
neat & with her own
not always predictable
route to travel

it's a pleasure just to wait
peer up the street
& here she comes
nimble & quick
but caring for kids
& polite to trucks

with small sneezes she stops
& glides me away
the only passenger
while the people outside
fall silent & take on colour
she has put them on tv
with the sound off
now nothing needs to be understood
& anyone might be a hero

behind the clear round
of her windows
through a still possible world
she carries me loving
& safe in herself

Davisville Rd., 1975

in the photo

above my desk
a gladiolus flaming in your lap
your face smiles at mine
my fingers hold
one crimson tongue

it is only hours
since your plane roared off
but i am back in the photo
cannot turn my eyes to yours
cannot reach
with singed fingers
another petal

Balliol St., 1976

zoos have bars

Your voice abstracts in a telephone
from melody to monotone
while me the instrument allows
only grunts and male meows
I need your eyes to shine my love on
This doesnt have your melon smell on
I want to squeeze real flesh and bone
unloosed from the clutch of a telephone.

Balliol St., 1976

fusion

no welding
of ores or floes
no liquation
of salt pillars
no sunthaw of drift
deliquescence of hardness
is like the melting
wherever my bones
fuse and dissolve
in your soft body
and we sleep into one
twinned and twined till we wake

and rise
still
welded

Toronto, March 1975

dream beyond death

from the dank pit
hand firm in hand
we walk up a sunfilled slope
the strange flowers above
bless us and beckon
escaped from time past
we are seven now both
i too am chinese
our obsidian eyes are bright
the fresh-peeled nectarines
in our cheeks

there is no need to talk
we know we are mounting at last
to our rightful life
waiting over the rim
we hear already the birds in song
we bring from our first world
only the one heart's pacer
we fashioned together

its pulse is lifting us now
to twice ten thousand days
we will have time at last
to become and beget
before fading
still loving
as one

i wake
and return to this vision
feeling our linked hands
more certain than all existence
this dream from desire is lava-deep
i cannot believe death's cold crater
will contain it

Scarboro Hospital, July 1975

moment of eclipse

moon slides
into our shadow
sun sucks
through our maw

owls hush
light dries
only the other suns flare

& the sudden fireflies
round this porch
coldly dancing

three thousand miles
beyond the curve of us
my love is walking
perhaps in sunshine

wordless your mouth
moves into mine

Uxbridge, Summer 1976

never blush to dream
(to a melody in the *Chrysanthemum Rag* of Scott Joplin)

1

never blush to dream
a lost love
slides into your bed again

there's no treason
though the blood stirs
when a stranger speaks his name

> each lover keeps the home
> he made within your mind
> and has a key
> to lie with you unbidden
> so long as you are holding
> gentle thoughts of him

2

never feel a guilt
to hear me
whisper still within the night

old loves lurk in eyes
that brighten
to the new enchanter's sight

> i too must rise from warmth
> to drift with other ghosts
> from worldly view
> yet i'll come into your bed
> some night again
> and dream myself alive in you

Toronto, 1977

fall in spring

i'm going to be real mad
if it dies
wai-lan sprays briskly
the potted rosebush
she womanhandled home for us
a crimson cloud
at easter

we wont let it
i say firmly
but i'm puzzled what alchemy
the local plantshop used
to trick this rambler
into april resurrection

'lan does not wonder
being twenty-seven
she believes
i can keep the sap alive
being seventy-two

after three days
the blossoms
wreathe our floor

Balliol St., 1977

dear biographer

there's a great snow-bank-job
in the university's MS collection
kept below melting
all the pleas boasts i love yous
snaps clips pix posters IOUs
sincerelys XXXes
everything insoluble in air
the world blew up around me

but the best friends
there was seldom need to write
and relatives had nothing to say

whatever was edible
dissolved long ago on the ghostly tongues
of perplexed parents
and frustrated teachers

a few books
but they are lies lacking nutrition
written by others
i once was   .

only my true love knows
what morsels are left
and she will not use them
to feed your image

University of Stirling, July 1977

bullfrog monolog

You'll find my Princess wintertime
bogged down in a swamp at York
but come summer she'll be singing
somewhere in grass by a waterside
Cwowk corse cwowk course i said 'singing'
she never croaks   like me
man she's a Princess
Rana pipiens   the meadow frog

Our very first night she sang me
the oldest Battrachian folksong
made music high and true
just for this lanky bullfrog
me   *Rana clamitans*

You probably think she's a green thing
to live with a wrinkled croaker like me
but *lawks* no she's pale brown
it's those crickety treefrogs are green
the chaps that go *qurrrrk qurrrrakk*
like a thumbnail over a comb
The Princess is beige and smooth
as an Anjou pear   pear without spot

Kwawtt what? Me sing? *Alawk* no
it's like those biologists say
"bullfrogs utter bass croaks and moans
though sometimes a piercing cry"
Yeah maybe i look pretty silly
hopping around on my big flat feet
the jowls on my belly quivering
though most times i'm sitting quiet
but busy   flip-flick   flip-flick
lassooing every bug in sight

There ought to be statues to frogs
We're the best friends of Man
of Dogs too   all you hotblooded fellows
We kill fleas flies gnats gnits
bugs mosquitoes no-see-ums
we're insecticidal maniacs
and no DDT needed

Kwowkh kwatt? 'Venomous'! Us?!
You've got us mixed with our distant cousins
way off at Toad Hall
and even they aren't 'venomous'
they won't give you warts
just a blister or two
though they've sure got enough to give away
Some toads are all wart
Still they're okay in a lumpish way
They flick a neat bug too
but not of course with our speed
and finesse
Kwort kwort? I *haven't gort worts —*
well one or two tiny ones
spawts more like
& the princess has absolutely none

Sure we think we're appealing
kwexy-wexy as we say
& we're known to be quite amorous
"A Frog he would a-wooing go, heigh ho!"
They don't sing that about toads
And what do those Greek frogs sing
when they make up a chorus?
Brek-ke-kek-kek ko-ax ko-ax
They're still singing it by the ponds in Crete
Sounds real sexy to me
the same tune our ancestors bobbed to
when they performed for Aristophanes
two thousand years and more ago
You don't believe me read his *Frogs*
a whole play about our Greek connection
Brek-ke-kek-kex the boys at Harvard
chant it still at ball games *ax* anybody

Krek-kroax krockle-chuckle   that's me now
& i can do *krowg-jowg jowg-krom*
jowg-o-rum   more rum!
that's pretty bacchanalian eh?

Ah but you must wait
till the Princess comes back
if you want to hear my piercing cry

Treehouse, May 1977

another bullfrog monolog

Sometimes when i'm the one
away from pond
i get feeling so insecure
i worry even about Mr. Toad

& that's a laugh
how could a bullfrog like me
lose his Princess to a toad?
We all know about toads i hope
how they're not a patch on frogs
can't sing a note
or swim worth a damsite
Sometimes they'll sit on the bottom of a swamp
just to show they're amphibians too
but mostly they just squat in grubby corners
whereas we're the athletes of the Two Worlds
Frogs were holding Battrachiads
before lungs even
hop-and-skip or broad
In our weight class we swim faster
than East Germans
Why we invented the breast-stroke
(you should see the Princess
a skinny-dipping beauty)
As for jumping
that old-timer in Calaveras County
Mark Twain said he coached
gets his record broken every year
Frogs never needed coaching
we'll jump yards just for the hell of it
But nobody's ever heard of a jumping toad.

So how could i be jealous of one?
Well it's this way:
the Princess & i feel sorry for toads
they're retarded but they're our kinfolk

So we run a benevolent society
the Toad Lovers' Club
& keep a kind of heraldic figure
a Totem Toad in our bedroom
He sits between our pillows

O he's just stuffed of course
with batten or something   plastic eyes
but they're very big & wistful
& his hide's real velvety & green
more like a frog's
except he's dumb & helpless
just sits there waiting for us

Or is it just for the Princess?
That's what i ask myself now i'm away

Still even Othello
& he was a real jealous type
wasn't suspicious of toads
In fact he thought they had no appetite
for anything   just brooded in wells
lived off vapour
no yen for love like us frogs

But Milton now he was more wary
thought there was a toad in Eden
"close at the ear of Eve"
& up to no good
Makes me wonder what people mean
when they say "toads complete a garden"
That toad was an agent for the Snake

Sure sure ours isn't real
an imaginary toad
but he's in a real Garden
& it's reserved for the Princess & me

I tell myself if Mr. Toad wasn't beside her
who knows what young pipsqueak *pipiens*
elegantly slim & amber-eyed
wouldn't be leaping around that pillow
spellbinding my Princess with his frogsong

I'm going to hop the next plane home

Toronto, August 1977

my love is young

my love is young & i am old
she'll need a new man soon
but still we wake to clip and talk
to laugh as one
to eat and walk
beneath our five-year moon

good moon   good sun
that we do love
i pray the world believe me
& never tell me when it's time
that i'm to die
or she's to leave me

Toronto, 1978

halfperson's day

halfawake on my side of the bed
my arm moves to emptiness
fumbles on Mr. Toad our Totem
lying stuffed & lugubrious
between me & the vacancy

there's only one peach to be peeled
one bowl one spoon one mouth
my red vitamin lacks a golden mate
one porch chair in the rising sun
the Globe turns in silence

to write is good perhaps
but her dark eyes flower above my page
i sound my scribbles in a solitude
the inner ear is only
halflistening

the telephone
"no. . . she'll be back in 13 days"
(plus 4 hours & 13 nights)

alone in the apartmenthouse pool
32 lengths   who cares?
back at the flat door i push my key
into our lock
withdraw to emptiness

wander to the piano
at least there's no one
to hear my mistakes
— but Mozart without her
is just a sit-up

so i do real sit-ups
or halfdo them
no one holding firm
to my good ankle

i take the partial body out
though walking's not a walk
a walk takes two takes me takes her

lie down at last in blackness
Toad's on the blanket still
too still   a limp perversion
beside a demiperson
plunging a schizophrenic head
into her pillow's almond bodysmell
i drown in something
yesterday we called our bed

Balliol St., 1977

diving

Loving you i hold my breath
i dive from dryness
slide to soft meadows
where all is upsidedownness
silence yielding
to silence

And then since love
is winged by words
wants air for launching
we heave aloft
are warmed in a glitter of sounds
that flake away with the wind

Loving you is beyond wings
is to sway with primal weed
is to dance with fins
in a joy too salt
for sounding

Toronto, 27 Jan. 1978

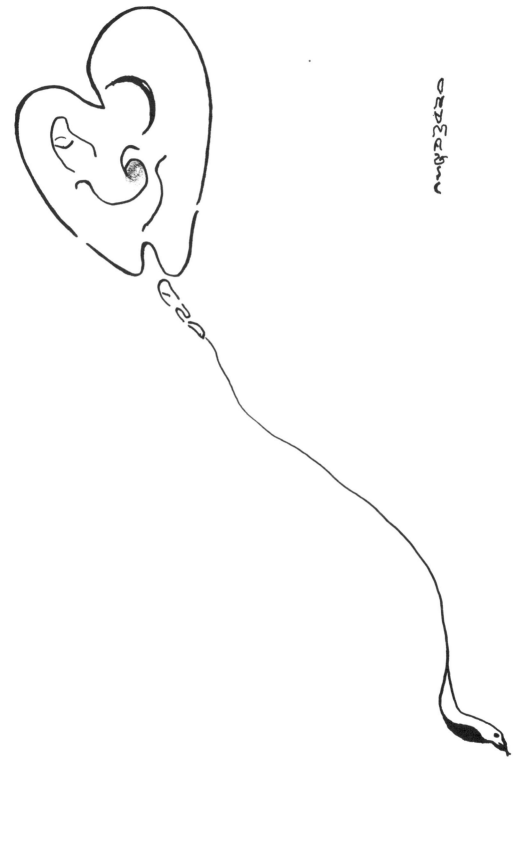

4
THE WIND
THROUGH ST. JOHN'S

January Morning/Downtown Vancouver

Dawn comes grey as a gull's wing

Between groaning foghorns
the first freighter's *basso profundo*
demands admission at the Lion's Gate

Trucks wake the dead alleys
downtown becomes hands on wheels
toes roaring motors
fingers triggering horns tempers

Heels quicken on pavements
soles shuffle at reds
jaws yawn then fix in waiting dreaming
come alive with green with buses
fall into rhythm with words gum cigarettes
Heads infinite in variety
absorb into buildings
mesh with repetition with keys
desks counters wheels receivers

The streets wait outside
chained to their hydrants
humming with wires tires talk
buildings' faces look down —
the glassy young expressionless
the old weathered into compassion
necklaced with concrete heraldry
or wearing bustles of wooden pillars
classical grimy   they hold up nothing

Whatever their characters they weep now
as rain twines through chipped granite
snakes down great panes
to patter on awnings cartops
and a sudden carnival of umbrellas bobbing

Rain stops   almost
Beyond the farthest ski-slope
a cyclops eye through cloud-crack
kindles the hats of hotels
glorifies antennae   the webs of bridges
bronzes the inlet
disappears

(The Park is dark wintergreen and drip
that stealthily mounts again to drizzle
chilling the fern and cedar
fir and salal and last year's grass
postponing the flowers
locked in the frosted earth)

the first hours are passing when money
is made   contacts reputations
bargains promises mistakes
trains phonecalls women men
made and unmade as the rain
rivers again
over meadows of glass
drips from the noses
of statues and under the cloud
cloaking the mountains
invisibly deepens to snow

Noon whistles over the millyards
Umbrellas tumble from doorways
bosoms are flattened by raincoats
Eating begins with drinking
juices martinis flattery
Celery is chewed   arguments briefings burgers
In the lanes pigeons patrol the backs of cafés
glaucous gulls are mewing over the harbour ships

The morning is gone

1972/77

song for a west coast february

O whether it is better
to stay a sloppy bachelor
wearing boots and yellow slicker
wading in the tears
of that soppy broad the weather

Or if a raincoat's better
galoshes and umbrella and
a beret or fedora
to settle down in wedlock
with this teeming wife the weather

Ambleside, B.C.

Moon down Elphinstone

Larry woke his girlfriend
  —Jan, your brother's smart.
Till this war's over
  I'm hidin out with Bart.

Larry took his compass,
  slid into his pack.
—When the shootin's over,
  love, we'll be back.

Moon up Mount Elphinstone
  lit a world of trees. . . .
Made it somehow through to Bart
  on feet, hands, knees.

Bart shot another squirrel,
  broiled it on a rack.
They crawled under blankets
  in their brushwood shack.

Moon down Elphinstone
  lit a world of bough.
—Bart, I just got to see
  what Jan's doin now.

Moon down the mountain
  bright going south,
but dark words only
  from her soft mouth.

—The war goes on and on, Larry.
   I'm only young now.
My new boy's comin to eat
   I dont want a row. . . .

Said the cop down in Skidroad—
   When you've slept off yer toot
you'll look a lot smarter
   in a noo khaki suit.

Day before his first leave
   the Sarge slung him the phone—
My ma's dyin, Larry;
   Bart should come home.

Sun on the tall firs,
   soldier up the slope.
—If Bart don't believe me
   he can read what Jan wrote.

Bart on the lookout snag
   sky building stormy.
—Only soldier I'm goin to kill
   is the one comin for me.

Deergun in the shadow,
   cap-badge in the light.
—Hafta send more than one
   to take me to fight. . . .

Bart turned him over,
   found his sister's note,
wrote P.S. in blood
   bright from Larry's throat:

—"Just dig a hole deep enough
   to bury me with him"
Cocked his gun, took a boot off,
   stuck the letter on a limb.

Rain down Elphinstone
   on bough, waves and shore,
on two boys' faces
   safe from a war.

Comox, B.C., 1951/Toronto, 1975

Prolog without Tales
(Toronto 1940)

When April slush has sloshed old March away
and like some storm-lost parakeet green May
has lit upon Toronto's slippery decks
then students write exams, and profs write cheques
to proof Muskoka shacks against mosquito
or fly to do research in Rome or Quito.
But student-grads mark papers until five,
drink beer on draft, and walk home to their wives.
At the end of such a day of Fails and Passes
there sat around two tables lush with glasses
some ten of us, with friends, in the Plaza cellar.

First was our Knight, a poet and a teller
of tales about Canadian beasts too human.
He was a dapper man, with some acumen;
when Bennett was P.M. he voted Tory;
his knighthood was a consequential glory.
His beard was trim, for nothing was newfangled,
and from his spectacles a ribbon dangled.
Gentle he was but with a roving eye.
He could be witty, but would never try
to damn another writer in our land,
though cause might be that most of them be panned.

With him he had a prioress, or such
she seemed. Her little lips would scarcely touch
the ritual ale the waiter brought. A lady
was she, meek of eye but not oldmaidy.
Her mouth seemed pursed in some ambiguous prayer
though she had ears like needles sharp to hear
Sir Charles's pearls and on the rosary
of memory thread them. Yet she was our one
essential guest. We would have had less fun
downing beers in the limbo of Men Only,
where womanless males were penned, remote and lonely.

A student of the law was with us, long
of nose and short of speech and seldom wrong.
Though he was modest and could manage tact,
he was from Yorkshire and intent on fact.
Brown ale he loved. He never slopped or smacked
and held his body poised though it was lanky.
His suit was grey, with matching tie and hanky.
Our weekend poker games he'd never missed;
he seldom raised and never was seen pissed.
Fresh articled was he to a firm downtown.
We all were sure he'd wear a scarlet gown
someday in Ottawa, nor were we wrong.

An advertising man we had who made
commercial rhymings for the perfume trade
yet hungered that by other deeds he might
be chosen heir-apparent to our Knight.
A kid-bound chapbook had he with him, printed
by hand on paper fine, the verse new-minted.
Copies he'd mailed to every maid and man
defined as authors in the *Who's Who (Can.)*
From it he hoped to read us patriot odes.
Round was his paunch and flabby as a toad's.
His round-glassed eyes were turning always, like
an owl's, to Sir Charles. His name was Mike
and none more quick than he to spot a waiter
and write our orders on the air, nor greater
memory had for quoting from Sir Chas.
His voice was high as choirboy at a Mass.
He knew all poets by the Christian name,
their wives as well. Alone Mike always came.

Today there sat with us a social worker.
Hard she worked and fought like any Ghurka
to find right fosterkin for babes deserted.
Big-thighed and -breasted was she, plainly skirted;
her throat was wide and resonant as a tuba;
she blew a laugh a man could hear in Cuba.
Her face was red and seamed as the City Hall
where soon she hoped to sit by the voters' call
as alderwoman bold, and tax the wealthy
to make more adults sane and children healthy.
She downed three beers without much ceremony;
divorced she was and drank on alimony.
A generous hand she had and loved to treat
the table. A merrier eye you'd never greet
although she suffered much from liver trouble.

A shadow came with her, though scarce a double,
a solemn girl in tweeds down to her feet.
A coke was all she'd drink but liked to eat
the Plaza's peanuts. To Oxford she had been
and now did book reviews. A pipe within
the corner of her mouth hardset she carried,
and wore a christy hat. She had not married
but was a fighter fierce for women's rights
and peace for all, except the Trotskyites.
Tersely she spoke, from the other side of her lip;
though frail of face she had a manly grip.

A bearded Aussie prof had newly joined
our group. With nose-ringed natives naked-loined
he'd lived for years, and though he lisped sometimes
Steve talked non-stop and downed his beers betimes.
He claimed he'd mastered six New Guinea tongues
and tort the bleeders English. Though his lungs
were wheezing now from snuffing hash with Mayas
he never ceased to lisp and cough and ply us
with oddball questions on Canadian folkways.
He peered out at our lawyer through the smokehaze
and asked if buggering the livestock ith
more common in the Praireeth than the Rockeeth.
Small he was yet bold and, more's the pity,
rash. His Head one day in a committee
queried Steve's updating of a *kris*.
The sword was brought. Steve swung it with a hiss
demanding that the Head choose any weapon
on the museum walls and end dispute the way
time-honoured by krith owners in Malay
(it leaves the loser with no leg to step on).
Steve's Head, however, picked a pen and fired him —
then next day, urged by all his staff, rehired him.

A salesman asked to join us who was lonely.
Today he'd pushed three hundred bells and only
sold, he said, one sub to *Saturday Night*.
He nursed the glass he'd brought until our Knight
persuaded him to let us buy his beers.
Glad he was and downed each pint with "Cheers!"
He told us he had never found a steady
job since leaving High. His grub and bed he
got most days from peddling door to door —
brushes, nightgowns, Bibles, soap. Before,
he was a butcher's boy, and now he thought
he'd join the airforce and, before he fought,
get butcher's training, rank and trade's pay
as well as keep and clothes and monthly payday.
Well-mannered was he with a shining eye
but doomed perhaps to sell less than he'd buy.

Our circle's edge held, always late, a student,
a zealous lad for truth, if seldom prudent.
His coat unpressed and salted all in dandruff,
with patches on each elbow and each cuff.
Of bottled ale he never had enough
if treated. Scorning to drink from glass or saucer
he'd toast us "bottles up!" Deep down in Chaucer
digging was he for a doctor's thesis.
Hot was his breath and smelt of cheeses.
A battered Chaucer text he'd always bring
—on every page a bottle-bottom ring—
and seek to teach us medieval grammar
by shouting *Troilus* out amid the clamour,
while empty bottles grew beside his arm.
And yet he had a reckless kind of charm.
His fags he rolled by hand with scarce a pause
but the more he drank the easier he was.

A wholesale merchant joined us for a quicky.
He ordered beer but spiked it from a mickey.
He listened much and carefully,
content to whisper fast asides to me
of this week's losses, gains and slidings,
carloads of lettuce left to rot on sidings
by railway strikers, Bay Street trading up.
Three years ago, competing for the Cup
the Undergrad Debaters offered he
had come to me for help in oratory.
His father then sold produce from a stall.
The son now owned ten trucks and a shopping mall.
I marvelled how from capital so small
my friend had raised his family's fortunes high
while his Professor-Doktor still must try
to live with wife on income one-tenth his.
But then, I thought, he'd always been a whizz
at charming profs and ladies, learning facts,
and figuring. If with the Devil he'd made pacts

he'd stayed an honest friendly lively wight.
Four hours, no more, he said he slept at night.
In truth I worked as hard at what I might
but what I might could help no starving man.
His shoes were shiny as a salesroom van,
his sober suit was of the finest weave.
He paid for ales around and smiling took his leave.

Late there joined us a cadet all hot
from afternoon parade. Though he had fought
upon the campus only, he would soon
he hoped command a Corps or a platoon
for downing Hitler. Tall he was and bony
as a sapling fir but limber as a pony.
A ladies' man he was, but wrapped in khaki,
the tunic come awry, the puttees tacky.
On half his head a wedge-cap bore a badge:
Arbor, its motto, *velut crescat*.
At parties he wore kilts and a tartan waistcoat.

There was a doctor with our house. He sported
a collar winged, a cane, bow-tie (imported),
a monocle, a pin of pearl, and in
his buttonhole a pink. I can't begin
to list his honours, private publications,
degrees and clubs, his lectures to the Asians,
his clinics, memberships on boards for culture,
billiards, opera, hockey, handball, sculpture.
Yet most of all he loved great poetry
and had financed Mike's chapbook. Always he
would help, he said, clean-bodied youths who wrote.
Whitman he loved, and Wilde, and he could quote
most Rupert Brooke and Fletcher's Hassan quite.
'Twas odd he spoke so little with our knight
and privately would say Canadian verse
was worth as much as a Hindu pauper's purse.
He was the leading surgeon in our town,
some said, and he agreed. Before each noun
he loved to put two adjectives or three.

With our merchant came a farmer who
was selling him what vegetables he grew.
He stayed to lift another Molson's ale.
His cheeks were round but weathered rough as Braille.
Knotted he was and big but stooped when standing.
From Holland had he come — to Holland Landing.
When asked he told us he grew corn and beet
enough to fill two barns, raised pigs for meat,
had thirty sheep in fold, twelve cows in stable,
two horses and a mule, and would be able,
he hoped, next year to build a house to hold
his wife, four kids, two sisters from the cold.
He planned a kitchen fitted out for meals and baking,
brewing beer, and jam and pickle-making.
His accent still was guttural but his speech
was more correct than any I might teach.
His eyes were calm and wise though baby blue.
He seemed a man this land would never rue.

That was our fellowship as of that day.
Our pardoner and friar were both away
together on a package tour to Rome.
Our carpenter had driven early home
on overtime to quaff his import ale
and listen by the radio to the game.
The dyer, miller, weaver did the same.
The shipman in a pub beside the harbour
was drunk already with the cook and barber.
The bursar, gazing out on campus trees,
was dreaming ways to up the student fees.
Closed was the haberdasher by his bank.
The parson and the plowman never drank.
Our Host, incorporate, could not materialize;
the Plaza's peanuts were our only pies.

And so, no Host, no tales, no tellers.
Come seven we'd been harried from the cellars
by hunger, poverty or saturation
to find each soul his separate habitation.

Our student grad, beneath the table found
his *Chaucer's Works*, the cover come unbound.
With tread unsteady Hart House towers he passed;
him thought their turrets merely mocked the Past,
cold mimes of all that world he longed for,
the craft from faith that to those times belonged.
He ate his evening cheeseburg in the Coop,
then joined a scattered scribbling group
of late-night readers in the library basement,
and sailed to his faery lands through a paper casement.

Epilog to a Prolog

In the spring of 1941 I was The Lecturer of the English Department in University College, Toronto, and a private-cadet in the university's army training corps. I would wind up my last seminar by four, change from customary teaching gown to required khaki, tramp around the quad juggling a rifle for an hour or so, then head for home on Hazelton. My battered feet would usually drag as I came abreast of the Park Plaza, and lead me into its basement beer parlour, the King Cole. This was a big room furnished with round tables in the centre, reserved for "ladies & escorts", and a dark rim of cramped accommodations for merely masculine drinkers. I soon learned that one or more tables in the middle were unofficially reserved for Sir Charles G. D. Roberts and his attendant ladies, and that lone males with any claim to literary or merely literate interests might attach themselves to his table. I was still under forty at this time and ambitious enough to think I might create a new Tabard of passing pilgrims from these encounters and furnish them with a new set of Canterbury Tales. The war, however, soon hustled me to more compelling scenes and companions. I stuffed away the prose notes I'd made — and dug them out thirty-six years later. Though it was obvious I'd never write the Plaza Tales, I thought I should at least try an abbreviated Prologue.

These resulting couplets obviously miss being Chaucerian by several light years, but the characters have perhaps a documentary interest in being, like Chaucer's, only about three-quarters fictional. And mine are shaped with the advantage of hindsight; I know what my prototypes became. There are the young ghosts here of a university president, a national pickle maker, a Justice of the Supreme Court. Some are long dead: the social worker, alas, and the Knight, and Mike and the doctor. The Aussie prof is a fusion of two quite different anthropologists who departed the Canadian scene for livelier adventures. A less charming version of the Chaucer student is still around.

the Wind through St. John's

Liquid steel the harbour stirs
is mercury under the Wind
    the Wind down Labrador from Baffin
    twisting always east
    in the top spin of our whirling world

bobbing the naked masts
of *Inacio Cunha* (Oporto 1970)
of *Elisabeth* (Fernando Po)
driven in from the Banks
a long roadstead of ships
and their crewmen jostling
    as the Basques were harried
    the *Guipuscoans*
    blown to these hard coves
    before Caboto   before Colombo
leaving their word for cod
on the lips of the Beothuk
and on Mercator's chart
terra de baccalos

Stripped of sail still they jump
the old hulks prance to the air's call
weave their sterns in a sarabande
of Maltese crosses
between Amerigo's oldest town
and the ocean's older maw

    This is the air a few days back
    that whistled around Pt. Barrow
    came over the Beaufort
    howling across the Boothia
    and over Hudson's Bay as once
    it howled over Hudson dead
    over Franklin dying
    and before them the first pre-Dorsets
    lasting it out in snowpits

Around the latest concrete towers
the storm blusters
and into the rocky throat
    the Labrador icecap drilled
    a few millennia back
    from the last peninsula out to the bed
    of that lost Champlain Sea

The gale mouths abrasion
thickens the dusk with scour
from the bloodred cliffs
licks dirt from the sprawling finger-pier
gnaws at the rust on the playground cannon
that once barked pirates away

This Wind that turns the Polar Cap
    elbowed the Vikings south to Vinland
    with crystals of ice bloodied their beards
    shouted Giovanni Caboto down from Belle Isle
    shoved Fagundes around Cap de Raz
    and John Rut home to England

Tonight it shreds green paint
from the jogging prow of another *Pinto*
rubbing through to the rib-patterns
that trail back to Polo's Venice

Over Signal Hill it climbs unflagged
unflagging   its messages only moans
through scrawny wires and the tatters of moss
unhooked and swirling over the cliffs
Spume rides through the dark
from the upcoast waves
spatters the Tower's memorial plaque
    that remembers newcomers
    blundering in from Bristol
    a mere five centuries back
    No epitaph for the bears
    or the Beothuks

an absence that never gives pause
to the illiterate Wind on the Hill
gouging a little deeper
the seaward scores of the ghost glacier
     vanished long before the Cabotos
     before Leif and Torvald
     and Bjarni killer of Skralings
     our glacier gone but not forgotten
     the Old One planning return
     But not as old as the western Wind
     that girdled whatever was north
     before even the oceans cooled
     and the plates of the world's hide drifted

In its own caprice the twining Wind
may puff this year safely to haven
all the boats bloody with skins of the doomed seal
or leave the clubbers to drift in fog
and be clubbed by the ice

This air
     that throbbed for Marconi
     bending to the first leap of speech over ocean
rides deaf to the east as ever
wordless beats against Europe
     as it beat back to their deaths
     who knows how many venturing Phoenicians
     what monks in a tub from Eire
     This is the passionless Gyre
     that held Cartier from harbour
     then let him furl his sails in an Avalon bay
     with time to kidnap a dozen *petites sauvages*
     and waft them back to France
     for a few more months of life

Four days and over Finistère
this gale may be shrieking
or storm the cliffs of Moher
and claw next week the Skerrymore light
or the empty Flannans
reeling to scatter the gannets
along the Butt of Lewis
sweeping Cape Wrath and Hoy
and booming the caves in Papa Stour

Racing now over St. John's tombs
and the fading glow in its patched heart
the Wind gyres into streets overlying
the footpath Sir Humphrey Gilbert took
for his last walk on land
It shakes the seaward shacks of the poor
and shifts to behead the last flowers
on the lawns of the darkened campus
In these gyrations the sea too is locked
and conspires with the sun
that set the lot of us twirling
  to fill this air with warmth and water
  and loose its force
  next month on the crags of Sumbo
  or leap in the ancient fury of levelling
  to inch the humps of Lofoten
  back to the seafloor

Tonight in a rift of the racing clouds
stars for a moment flicker
over pre-Cambrian cliffs that shelter now
the cocktail lounge of the Pink Poodle
See where a satellite creeps
in this cloudgap whispering perhaps
in private to lonely towers and tossing freighters
whatever the tale of tempests to come
  whispering till it too is pulled down
  somewhere by the earth's weight
  to burn into dust for the Wind
squalling now on Cape Spear and into these toy
galleons dancing

the Wind that will go bellowing
over Cape Farewell and frosted Nordkapp
the captious Wind that drowned Chancellor
and spared Ottar a millennium back
to tell King Alfred the first tale
of great whales and walrus waiting
to die that men might be rich

Beyond Novaya Zembla
beyond the packice in the Leptev Sea
the Wind will sweep
as it swept over Bering's bones on Wrangel
and skimmed the polar ice to Amundsen's Gulf
polishing Hearne's name on a Coppermine rock
and come again declaiming through St. John's town
saying nothing

saying only that air and earth and sea will be one
and whirl in the Sun
within the reeling Circle

Newfoundland, 1977

prayer

our father who art
the positive particle's
particle
forgive us not
our daily increase
as we forgive not the other species

lead us not into further complexity
but deliver us
from ourselves

for thy atom will re-form
and thy pulsing be somewhere done
in life as in death

for whatever is ever
with or without
us

Eire, May 1977

Acknowledgements

To the Canada Council, for aid and encouragement leading to the making of some of these pieces

To Oberon Press, Canada, for the reprinting of two visuals from *Four Parts Sand*, 1972

To Marty Gervais & his Black Moss Press for nine makings from *The Rugging & the Moving Times*, Coatsworth, 1976

To Jamie Hamilton & his Pikadilly Press for six visuals from *Alphabeings*, London, Ont., 1976

To the following periodicals:

> Hydra, Greece; *S.H.Y.*
> London, England: *Ambit; New Poems / 1976; Outposts*
> U.S.A.: *Happiness Holding Tank; Quartet; Western Humanities Review*
> Canada: *Antigonish Review; Blewointment; Canadian Forum; Capilano Review; Cross Country; CV II; elfinplot; event; Georgia Straight; Mainline; Matrix; Northern Journey; Ontario Review; Quarry; Repository; Rikka; Saturday Night; Tamarack Review; 3¢ PULP; Waves; West Coast Review.*

To Nexus & the Canadian Broadcasting Corporation for the first airing of "Never Blush to Dream", 1977